Curious and Fantastic Creatures

DOVER PUBLICATIONS, INC.
New York

Bibliographical Note

This Dover edition, first published in 1995, is a republication of the illustrations from *Les Songes Drolatiques de Pantagruel,* as described in the Publisher's Note.

DOVER *Pictorial Archive* SERIES

This book belongs to the Dover Pictorial Archive Series. You may use the designs and illustrations for graphics and crafts applications, free and without special permission, provided that you include no more than ten in the same publication or project. (For permission for additional use, please write to: Permissions Department, Dover Publications, Inc., 180 Varick Street, New York, N.Y. 10014.)

However, republication or reproduction of any illustration by any other graphic service, whether it be in a book or in any other design resource, is strictly prohibited.

Library of Congress Cataloging-in-Publication Data

Songes drolatiques de Pantagruel. English
   Curious and fantastic creatures.
      p.   cm. — (Dover pictorial archives series)
   Republication of the illustrations from Les Songes drolatiques de Pantagruel, which first appeared in 1565: reproduced here from the 1869 ed. published by Librairie Tross, Paris. Les Songes drolatiques de Pantagruel illustrated themes from F. Rabelais' Pantagruel.
    ISBN 0-486-28463-8 (pbk.)
   1. Songes drolatiques de Pantagruel—Illustrations.   2. Rabelais. François, 1490–1553? Pantagruel.—Illustrations.   3. Caricatures and cartoons—France—History—16th century.   4. French wit and humor. Pictorial.   I. Rabelais, François, 1490–1553? Pantagruel. II. Title. III. Series.
NC1493.S6713   1995
741.5'944—dc20

94-42781
CIP

Manufactured in the United States of America
Dover Publications, Inc., 31 East 2nd Street, Mineola, N.Y. 11501

Publisher's Note

In 1565, 12 years after the death of Rabelais, there appeared a volume of illustrations entitled *Les Songes Drolatiques de Pantagruel, ou sont contenues plusiers figures de l'invention de maistre François Rabelais: & derniere oeuvre d'iceluy, pour la recreation des bons esprits* ("The humorous dreams of Pantagruel, wherein are contained many figures from the imagination of master François Rabelais: & his last work, for the amusement of good spirits"). The original, for which none of the uncredited drawings survive, was published by Richard Breton, Paris. The present edition is reproduced from the facsimile printed by W. Drugulin, Leipzig, and published by Librairie Tross, Paris, 1869. For reasons of space, the pages have been reformatted.

The exact meaning of the drawings is unclear, and has been debated by scholars. Some claim it is political and satirical, holding, for example, that the likeness of Pope Julius II appears no less than twenty-one times. These are considerations for scholars. This edition is intended to make available to the public the extremely imaginative, pungent illustrations.

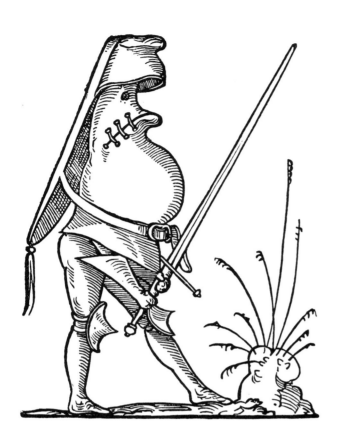

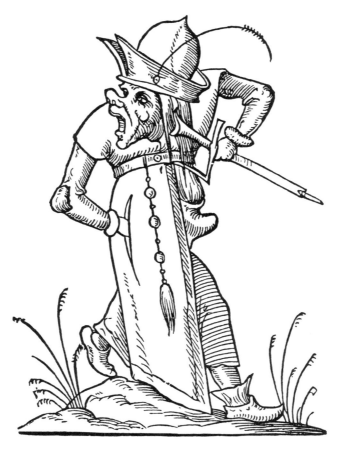

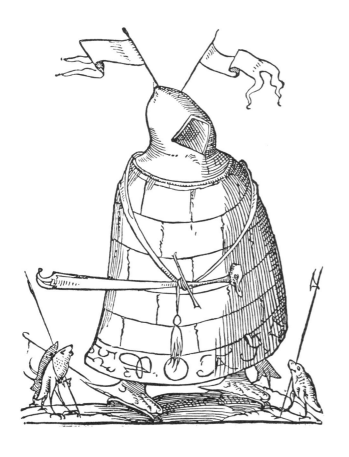

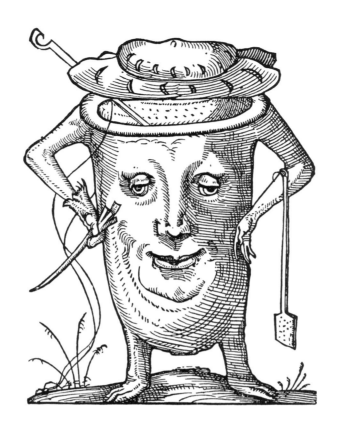

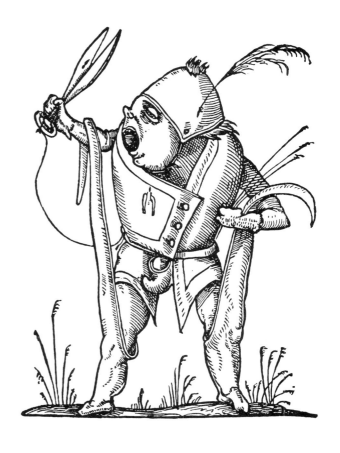

13

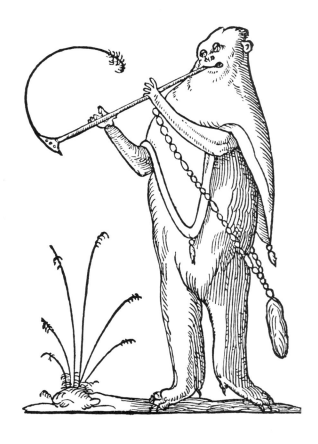

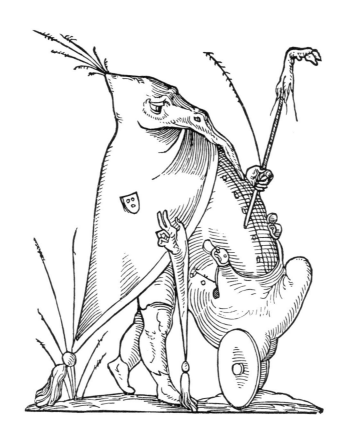

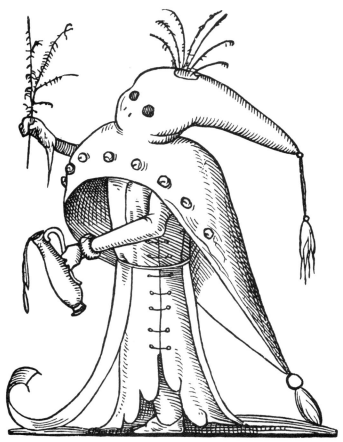

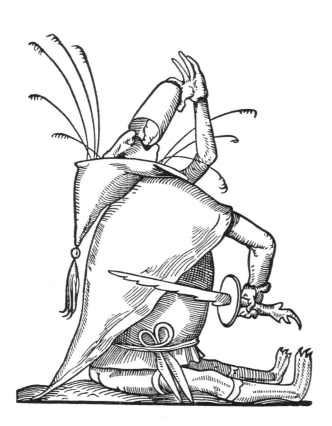

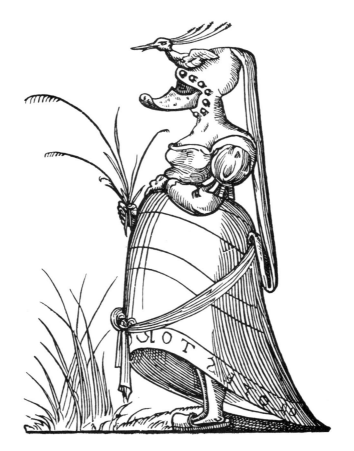

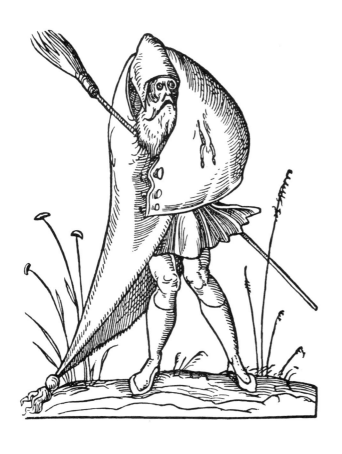

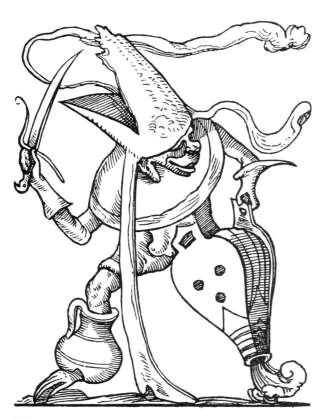

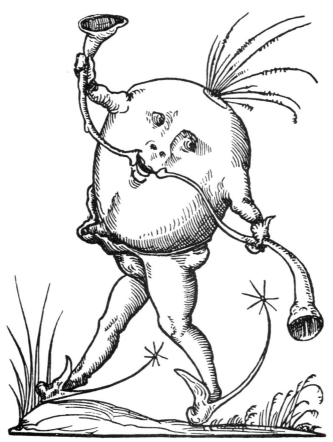

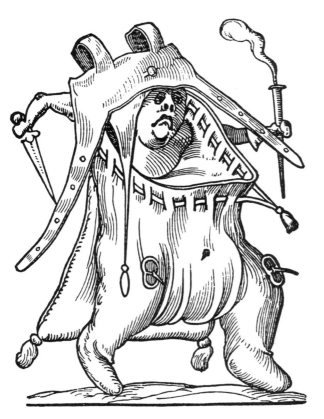

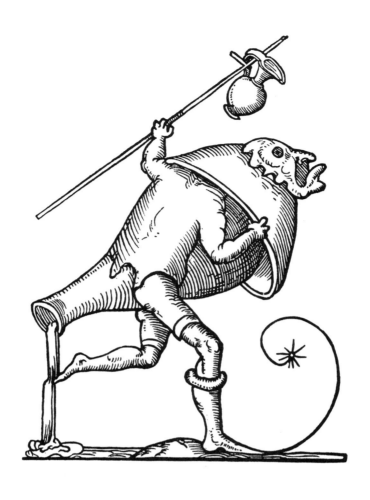

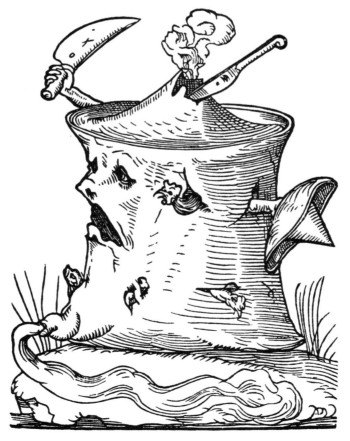

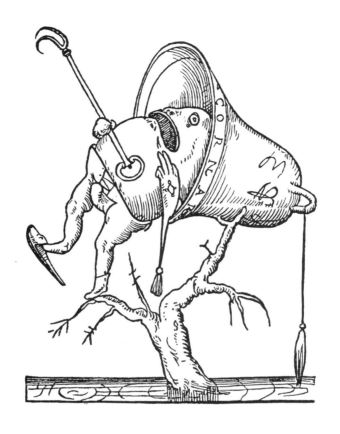

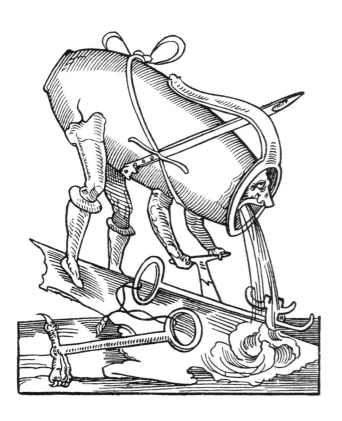